THE NORTH STAFFORDSHIRE OATCAKE is the gastronomic symbol of the region and the local fast food ~ still served from a host of little 'oatcake shops' throughout the area.

But despite its local popularity, the history of the oatcake is shrouded in mystery Some say it came from British Colonial India ~ a distant cousin of the Asian flatbreads ~ brought home by returning soldiers of the North Staffordshire Regiment. Perhaps the oatcake was inspired by the humble French crepe? Its most likely origins, however, are probably more local, a natural consequence of growing oats on the bleak upland farms of the Staffordshire Moorlands; made of oatmeal, flour, milk, water, sugar and a little yeast, the farmers had all the ingredients to hand for an energy rich meal. The 'bakestones' of the farmhouse industry would have evolved into the griddles used to cook oatcakes in the modern shops, from where they are served warm, filled with cheese and bacon, or sausage.

Take an area rich in natural beauty ~ rolling hills to the west, high gritstone crags to the east with limestone hills beyond. Impose an early industrial revolution driven by rich subterranean resources ~ carboniferous clays, coal measures and ironstones from which arose great potteries, coal mines and iron foundries; fulfil the need for efficient transport by building canals which overcame huge engineering challenges, followed one hundred years later by railways. Then allow nature to reclaim and man to preserve and the result is one of England's most fascinating - and for the most part picturesque - regions. In North Staffordshire history exists around every corner ~ or, more appropriately, over every hill!

In a series of short walks this guide explores some of the more characterful aspects of North Staffordshire's history, from the town centres of Stoke and Burslem through rural villages such as Cheddleton and Barlaston to special tours of great engineering projects such as the Harecastle Tunnels, Knypersley Reservoirs, Etruria and the massive Hazelhurst aqueduct. No walk exceeds two miles in length, and the maps are of such detail that no route instructions are required, leaving room for illustration and historical commentary.

Between each walk is a feature article on a nearby venue or theme which has special historical significance, from the medieval origins of Trentham Gardens to the magical beauty of Rudyard Lake. From the Elizabethan manor at Ford Green Hall to the Potteries Rail Loop, now converted into a series of greenways......

RAMPARTS AND TWO ROUND TOWERS are all that remain of Chartley Castle near Uttoxeter, built in the early 13th century by Ranulph Blundeville, 6th Earl of Chester. Mary Queen of Scots was held prisoner here before meeting the headman's axe on the 8th February 1587, at Fotheringhay. At the time Chartley Castle was the seat of the 2nd Earl of Essex - a favourite of Elizabeth 1 until he outgrew her affections and was also beheaded. Chartley then passed to his son, Richard Devereux, 3rd Earl of Essex, who went on to become a famous Cromwellian leader. A rare breed of cattle roamed free in this park for 700 years; descended from the primitive aurochs first domesticated by the Romans; Chartley Cattle are now preserved outside the county.

2

Principally, this is a guide which explores the history of North Staffordshire "on the ground", created for those who enjoy combining the excitement of discovery with the delight of walking. It has been a wonderful project to research and draw, a labour of love and an excuse to get "out and about" in the county in which I live. Jake~ my ever enthusiastic Field Spaniel~ loved the walking too!

Everything in this book is by hand ~ illustrations, maps and text are all drawn to create a series of themed compositions which I hope are pleasing on the eye as well as useful. Credit, then, is also due to Nick Reardon, my publisher, who has taken my raw fifty pages and turned them into this finished book. Nick and I have worked together for ten years and his publishing expertise is an asset.

I have tried to balance rural and urban themes, and in so doing one soon finds that the great townships of North Staffordshire overflow with such remarkable history. With that theme in mind, please await Volume 2!

TWO BOTTLE OVENS reflected in the Trent and Mersey Canal in Hanley were built in 1887 for Cliff Vale Potteries.

WEDGWOOD VISITOR CENTRE Barlaston

is the third location for a Wedgwood factory. Josiah was born in Burslem where he opened his first pottery in 1759. (see walk 4). A scientist, artist and engineer, he revolutionised the pottery industry, creating original new products of a quality and style not previously seen. Ten years later he opened a new factory in Etruria (see walk 3) and created the concept of a self contained industrial community ~ a modern factory, good housing for his potters, and a location chosen so he could pioneer canal transport. Two and a half centuries later, and after moving from Etruria to Barlaston Park in 1936, the Wedgwood Visitor Centre allows us to tour the production process, together with shops, restaurants and a museum.

Josiah Wedgwood

THE WEDGWOOD FACTORY drawn from the Trent and Mersey Canal. Josiah Wedgwood actively supported the creation of this canal in order to transport his finished pottery, and his incoming ingredients, faster, more cheaply and more carefully.

WEDGWOOD & BARLASTON

2 miles. Terrain: canal towpath, field walking *(with stiles)* and roads.

WEDGWOOD AND BARLASTON became synonymous in 1936 when the Wedgwood Company relocated their Etruria factory to Barlaston Park. We tour the park and explore the history of the village, so closely connected to the Trent and Mersey Canal and the North Staffordshire Railway. The Wedgwood factory has a famous visitor centre with shops and restaurants.

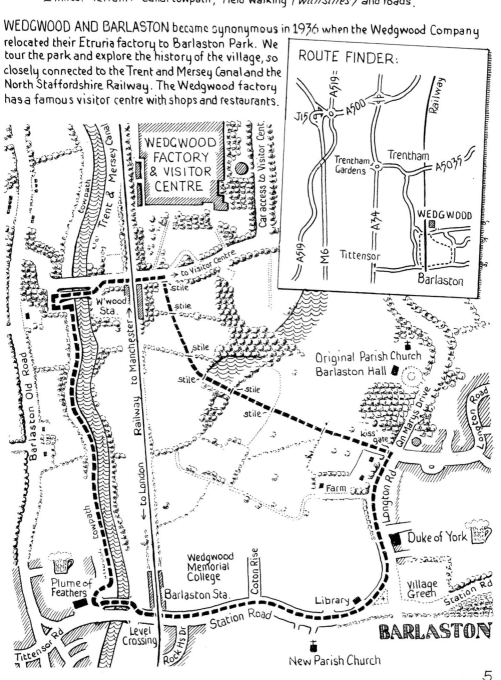

TRANSPORT VALLEY: canal, road and rail run parallel through the Trent Valley:

BARLASTON OLD ROAD linked Stone with Newcastle and was originally the great main road linking London with the North West. However the lowlying road was frequently flooded by the River Trent so was abandoned in favour of a new road ~ the current A34 ~ on the far side of the valley.

THE TRENT AND MERSEY CANAL winds through open countryside in Barlaston which belies its commercial origins. Josiah Wedgwood provided finance and encouragement for the construction of the canal between 1766 and 1777, and this money was well invested; the canal was largely responsible for the growth and development of the Potteries as an industrial centre.

THE NORTH STAFFORDSHIRE Railway ('the Knotty') opened the railway through Barlaston in 1848~9 to bring the national rail network into the Potteries.

THE DUKE OF YORK is one of two village pubs on the tour. 200 years ago as a row of four cottages but now ...ves good food and ale; a warm ...elcome awaits in the lounge ...d bar adorned with beams and horse brasses. Despite the modern appearance ...f the Plume of Feathers it too is an ancient inn; it was here at least at the time the Trent and Mersey Canal was being built.

NEW PARISH CHURCH adjoins Barlaston's village green

HILLTOP LANDMARK: clearly visible from both the M6 and the A34, Barlaston Hall stands guard over its parkland from a ridge high above the Trent Valley. From here there are views west towards the Hanchurch Hills and north to Stoke-on-Trent. Built in 1756 by Thomas Mills ~ a wealthy lawyer from Leek ~ it seems probable that the vast Barlaston Park was laid out at the same time, including the series of lakes we see today. During World War II this hall became ~ temporarilly ~ the headquarters of the Bank of England, in association with nearby Trentham which hosted the London Clearing Banks. Next door stands the original Barlaston Parish Church, abandoned in 1980 due to mining subsidence.

A TRANQUIL VIEW of the village green. Barlaston grew up around its green, and the picturesque white washed building on the left was once the Village School. Established at the end of the 18th century by Thomas Mills of Barlaston Hall, it flourished until 1967 when it was replaced by a larger, more modern building. It is now a library and, in an inspired innovation, occasionally serves coffee.

BRONZE STATUES of Perseus and Medusa, cast in 1847, guard the 70 acre lake. *(drawn during Stoke Show, hence the cars on display)*

THE HISTORY OF TRENTHAM GARDENS begins at the close of the 7th century when Wulfhere, King of Mercia from AD 659-674, ruled his Kingdom from a 'castle' or 'camp' three miles south of here at Bury Bank. Wulfhere's daughter, Werburgh, founded a Nunnery on the banks of the River Trent, on the site upon which Trentham Church now stands. Werburgh's first Church was probably destroyed by Viking invaders but from the Domesday Survey of 1087 it is apparent that a new Church had been built here, possibly by Elfleda, daughter of Alfred the Great, in the early 10th cent. Trentham continued as a major religious Priory until 1536 when it was dissolved by King Henry VIII and the estate sold to the Duke of Suffolk. St Mary's Church in Trentham *illustrated right*, however, is built on the foundations of both Werburgh's and Elfleda's Churches. In 1540, two years after the dissolution, the estate was sold to James Leveson. As one era finished, so another began .....

Werburgh

King Wulfhere, AD 660

8

TRENTHAM GARDENS

TRENTHAM PARISH CHURCH, drawn from the Italian gardens, has been a site of continuous Christian worship since the 7th century. The Norman pillars of the earlier Augustinian Priory were incorporated into the present Church, designed by *Barry* and completed in 1844.

....SO TRENTHAM PARK was sold in 1540 to James Leveson, whose successors the Leveson-Gowers, later to become the Dukes of Sutherland, enlarged and landscaped it so that by the mid 19th cent Trentham was a vast Italianate mansion surrounded by formal gardens. The house was built in 1833–42 by *Sir Charles Barry*, architect of the Houses of Parliament whilst the large lake had been proposed in 1759 by *Capability Brown*. On a hill to the south is a column supporting a statue of the 1st Duke of Sutherland erected in 1836. It was the industrialisation of the Potteries and the ensuing of the River Trent which forced the Leveson-Gowers to leave Trentham, and their house was demolished in 1912.

George Granville Leveson-Gower   'Capability' Brown

9

TWO SEMI CIRCULAR ARCHES AND TWO PIERS in the garden of Stoke's Perpendicular Church form a dramatic reconstruction of the original medieval Church. Potteries antiquarian Charles Lynam discovered the stones in the race of Bootham Mill when it was demolished in 1881 and determined to use them as a memorial to the ancient centre of worship. The low, square pavement in front of the arches is Josiah Wedgwood's grave. Rising above the trees is the new Church, consecrated in 1830 and containing a Saxon font and memorial tablets to three great local potters ~ Josiah Wedgwood, Joseph Spode and John Bourne.

THE IMPRESSIVE STOKE TOWN HALL was begun in 1834 with the two wings added in 1842 and 1850. Originally the ground floor of the central area was built for a covered market, with a cattle market in the yard behind, but in 1888 it was converted into the Council Chamber. Constructed of huge stone blocks with a giant portico of Ionic arches, the massive scale of this building must have dwarfed all around it in the mid-nineteenth century. In 1910-11 the King's Hall was added behind, and is still a dance venue today.

CENTRAL STOKE

1 mile. Terrain: largely street walking.

THE TOWN OF STOKE gave its name to the City of Stoke-on-Trent ~ initially because of its ecclesiastical supremacy as the controlling Parish of the area, and later as the City's administrative centre. But it was not always so; in 1780, when Burslem was already a hive of industry, Stoke consisted of one Church and five houses! The reason was the 'Glebe Lands' - 150 acres of low lying marshland owned by the Church and not developed until two canals were routed through what is now Stoke town centre. Whereas the earliest potteries had been high above Stoke in Penkhull, the new factories were now built near the canals in the valley below: Spode has been making china in the centre of Stoke since 1770. We tour the heart of this town ~ exploring the history of its Church, its canals, its great potteries and its railway, meeting en route some very characterful buildings.

The FOWLEA BROOK ran underneath the Newcastle Canal giving AQUEDUCT STREET its name

The rise in the road at this junction allowed the NEWCASTLE CANAL to pass underneath. Opened in 1797, it ran 4 miles from Newcastle-under-Lyme to its junction with the T & M here in Stoke. Its final demise came with the construction of the A500 in 1970.

THE LIBRARY was built in 1878 by Charles Lynam

Portmeirion

STOKE MARKET was designed in 1883 by Charles Lynam whose architectural work led him to rebuild the arches to Stoke's original Church in the Churchyard

SAINSBURY'S SUPERMARKET stands on the site of the old Minton Pottery; a statue of Colin Minton Campbell is outside.

GLEBE STREET was laid out in 1830 on land which was originally the 'Glebe Estate' - 150 acres belonging to the Church. Both the old Church and the Rectors house ~ Stoke Hall which stood roughly on this site ~ were moated to provide protection from the River Trent which occasionally flooded across this low lying meadow. The old Stoke Parish Church did not stand on this site - the present Church was built here in 1826-29 and is interesting for its many monuments, many of which were removed from the old Church.

Map labels:

North Stafford Hotel
Statue of Josiah Wedgwd
Winton Square
Stoke Rlwy Sta.
A52 to Leek
Junction of Newcastle and T & M Canals
Station Rd
A500
Copeland St.
Leek Rd A52
Fowlea Brook
Lytton Street
Trent and Mersey Canal
Elenora Street
Vehicle entrance
Civic Centre
Aqueduct St
SPODE
Liverpool Rd.
Hartshill Road
One time route of Newcastle Canal
Pedestrian entrance
Kingsway
Kings Hall
Town Hall
War Mml
Glebe Street
Brook St
St Peter Ad Vincula
Arches from original Church
Josiah Wedgwd's tomb
A500
Church Street
Route of NEWCASTLE CANAL with a branch into Minton's Pottery works
South Wolfe St.
London Road
Fleming Road
A5006 Lonsdale Street
Church St.

SPODE is the longest established working pottery in England. Founded in 1770 by Josiah Spode, who as a six year old boy had watched his father buried in a pauper's grave, this pottery was catapulted to success by two early discoveries. First, in 1784, Josiah perfected the process of blue underglaze printing on earthenware. He then made what was arguably the most important discovery in the history of the pottery industry ~ the formula for Fine Bone China ~ for which Josiah Spode achieved world fame. Today the Spode factory, visitor centre, shops and museums are still on the same site, here in Stoke.

THE WONDERFULLY "WALT DISNEY-ESQUE" building opposite the Town Hall is ' 1 Brook St ', built in Tudor Gothic style in 1867, and once a branch of the National Provincial bank . Brook Street crosses the culverted Fowlea Brook .

SIR OLIVER LODGE *(1851-1940)* was born in Stoke. As the first man to transmit a message by wireless he achieved world fame, and went on to invent electric spark ignition .

12

RAILWAY SPLENDOUR: arguably the most aesthetic Victorian building in Staffordshire, Stoke-on-Trent Railway Station opened in 1848 to great public acclaim. Its imposing frontage is Tudor-esque with gabled wings projecting from each end, whilst on the ground floor a Tuscan colonnade of seven arches welcomes passengers into the booking hall. This was also the headquarters of the North Staffordshire Railway, and the square bay on the first floor was their boardroom; its oak panelled walls and plaster moulded ceiling reflecting the confidence of the early railway entrepreneurs.

Across the tree lined Winton Square a hotel was also created-now the North Stafford- built in the style of an Elizabethan manor house to echo the theme of the station opposite. And in the centre of Winton Square stands a bronze statue of Josiah Wedgwood by Edward Davis in 1863; note how Josiah, true to his non-conformist principles, has his back to the licenced hotel premises! Instead he faces the station and his beloved canal~both symbols of industrial progress.
Illustrated: North Stafford Hotel and statue.

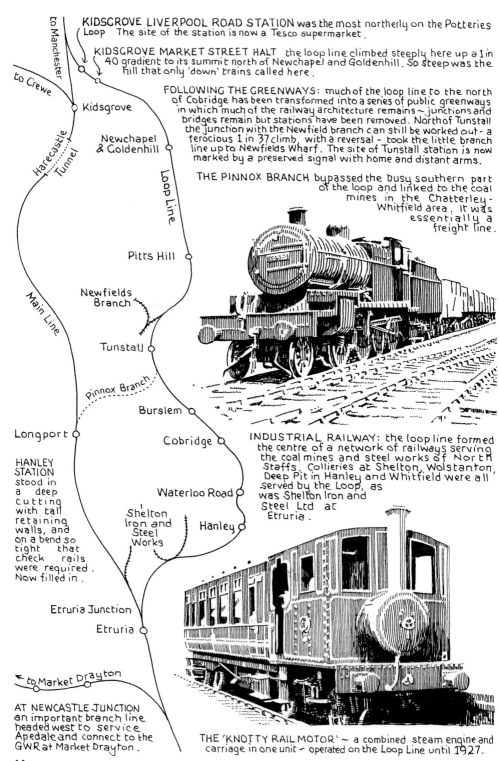

KIDSGROVE LIVERPOOL ROAD STATION was the most northerly on the Potteries Loop. The site of the station is now a Tesco supermarket.

KIDSGROVE MARKET STREET HALT the loop line climbed steeply here up a 1 in 40 gradient to its summit north of Newchapel and Goldenhill. So steep was the hill that only 'down' trains called here.

FOLLOWING THE GREENWAYS: much of the loop line to the north of Cobridge has been transformed into a series of public greenways in which much of the railway architecture remains ~ junctions and bridges remain but stations have been removed. North of Tunstall the junction with the Newfield branch can still be worked out - a ferocious 1 in 37 climb, with a reversal - took the little branch line up to Newfields Wharf. The site of Tunstall station is now marked by a preserved signal with home and distant arms.

THE PINNOX BRANCH bypassed the busy southern part of the loop and linked to the coal mines in the Chatterley-Whitfield area. It was essentially a freight line.

to Manchester

to Crewe

to Manchester

Kidsgrove

Newchapel & Goldenhill

Harecastle Tunnel

Loop Line

Pitts Hill

Newfields Branch

Main Line

Tunstall

Pinnox Branch

Burslem

Longport

Cobridge

HANLEY STATION stood in a deep cutting with tall retaining walls, and on a bend so tight that check rails were required. Now filled in.

Waterloo Road

Shelton Iron and Steel Works

Hanley

INDUSTRIAL RAILWAY: the loop line formed the centre of a network of railways serving the coal mines and steel works of North Staffs. Collieries at Shelton, Wolstanton, Deep Pit in Hanley and Whitfield were all served by the Loop, as was Shelton Iron and Steel Ltd at Etruria.

Etruria Junction

Etruria

← to Market Drayton

AT NEWCASTLE JUNCTION an important branch line headed west to service Apedale and connect to the GWR at Market Drayton.

THE 'KNOTTY RAIL MOTOR' ~ a combined steam engine and carriage in one unit - operated on the Loop Line until 1927.

THE POTTERIES RAILWAY LOOP

TUNSTALL STATION: a train bound for Stoke-on-Trent waits on the southbound platform.

THE POTTERIES LOOP LINE opened in 1875 to service some of the most densely populated areas of Stoke-on-Trent. The main north~south railway - opened 26 years earlier~ was busy and ran too far west of Tunstall, Cobridge, Burslem and Hanley. The creation of this urban railway was thus a great success, running 20 trains each day until the Second World War, but it was not to last. Eventually competition with road transport became too great and passenger services were withdrawn in 1964.

Freight provided an equal justification for the Potteries Loop; growing industries to the east of the region required access to the railway network which was achieved by laying a series of branch lines off the main loop. Freight rolled on until 1967 when the Loop was finally closed and track lifting began, although a partial reprieve from '71-'76 served Park Farm open mine.

Today much of the Loop has been converted into a series of public 'greenways' for walking and cycling (see illustration ←).

DIRK BOGARDE starred in the 1952 film 'Hunted' whose railway scenes were filmed on Burslem Station

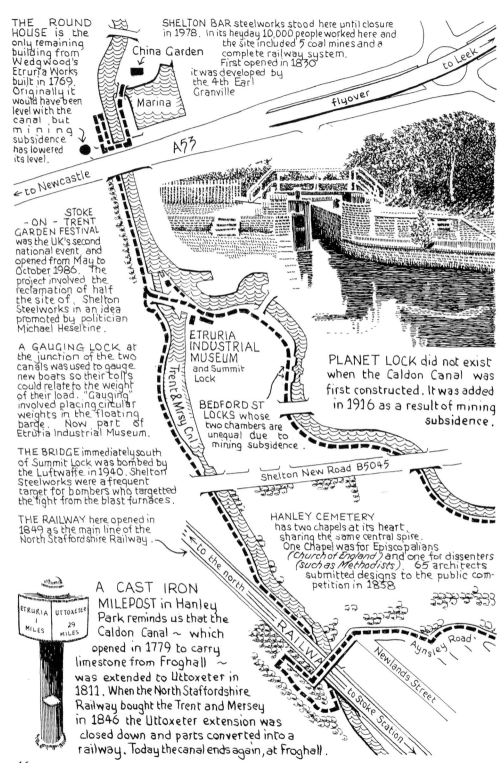

THE ROUND HOUSE is the only remaining building from Wedgwood's Etruria Works built in 1769. Originally it would have been level with the canal, but mining subsidence has lowered its level).

China Garden

Marina

SHELTON BAR steelworks stood here until closure in 1978. In its heyday 10,000 people worked here and the site included 5 coal mines and a complete railway system. First opened in 1830 it was developed by the 4th Earl Granville

to Leek

flyover

A53

← to Newcastle

STOKE - ON - TRENT GARDEN FESTIVAL was the UK's second national event, and opened from May to October 1986. The project involved the reclamation of half the site of, Shelton Steelworks in an idea promoted by politician Michael Heseltine.

A GAUGING LOCK at the junction of the two canals was used to gauge new boats so their tolls could relate to the weight of their load. "Gauging" involved placing circular weights in the floating barge. Now part of Etruria Industrial Museum.

THE BRIDGE immediately south of Summit Lock was bombed by the Luftwaffe in 1940. Shelton Steelworks were a frequent target for bombers who targetted the light from the blast furnaces.

THE RAILWAY here opened in 1849 as the main line of the North Staffordshire Railway.

ETRURIA INDUSTRIAL MUSEUM and Summit Lock

Trent & Mrsy Cnl

BEDFORD ST LOCKS whose two chambers are unequal due to mining subsidence.

PLANET LOCK did not exist when the Caldon Canal was first constructed. It was added in 1916 as a result of mining subsidence.

Shelton New Road B5045

HANLEY CEMETERY has two chapels at its heart, sharing the same central spire. One Chapel was for Episcopalians (Church of England) and one for dissenters (such as Methodists). 65 architects submitted designs to the public competition in 1858

to the north

RAILWAY

ETRURIA 1 MILES

UTTOXETER 29 MILES

A CAST IRON MILEPOST in Hanley Park reminds us that the Caldon Canal ~ which opened in 1779 to carry limestone from Froghall ~ was extended to Uttoxeter in 1811. When the North Staffordshire Railway bought the Trent and Mersey in 1846 the Uttoxeter extension was closed down and parts converted into a railway. Today the canal ends again, at Froghall.

Aynsley Road

Newlands Street

to Stoke Station →

ETRURIA TO HANLEY PARK

2 miles.   Terrain: canal towpath, parkland and a little street walking.

ALTHOUGH THIS WALK is close to Hanley centre, it connects a series of green spaces and has the ambience of a rural waterside stroll. Etruria was created by Josiah Wedgwood in 1769 – a revolutionary concept as a self contained industrial community ~ built alongside James Brindley's Trent and Mersey Canal. Here too stood the massive Shelton Bar steelworks whose site became Festival Park after the National Garden Festival of 1986. Passing Etruria junction and the Industrial Museum, this walk climbs the Caldon Canal past Staffordshire's only staircase locks to reach Hanley Park, recently improved, the returns via the Trent and Mersey and the canalside Hanley Cemetery.

Etruria Junction

A BRONZE STATUE OF JAMES BRINDLEY overlooks Etruria junction from the grounds of the Beth Johnson sheltered housing complex. Although a man of little formal education, James Brindley's inventiveness and capacity for hard work made him one of the UK's major canal designers, eventually responsible for 375 miles of waterway.

Born near Chapel-en-le-Frith he set up his own mill in Leek in 1742, then moved north to tackle a tough engineering problem at a Lancashire colliery. His ingenious work brought him to the attention of the Duke of Bridgewater, who employed him to build the 'Duke's Cut' canal in 1759; after more ingenious solutions, Brindley was asked to design the Trent and Mersey Canal by a group of entrepreneurs including Josiah Wedgwood. The work took 8 years to complete, but sadly Brindley did not live to see it finished: he contracted pneumonia whilst surveying the route of the Caldon Canal and died in 1772. By 1790 the Trent and Mersey canal was at the heart of a network linking every major UK river.

JESSE SHIRLEY'S Etruscan Bone and Flint Mill was built in 1857 to grind materials for the pottery industry. Served by a basin off the Trent & Mersey Canal (illustrated) it is strategically located to make the best use of canal transport. This is Britain's sole surviving steam powered potter's mill and contains an 1820's beam engine called Princess; it is now part of Etruria Industrial Museum.

Bedford Street locks are Staffordshire's only staircase locks, and are unequal due to mining subsidence.

HANLEY PARK was designed by Thomas Mawson in 1892 although the landscaping took five years to complete. The Caldon Canal runs through the park but was originally hidden from view so the working boats wouldn't spoil the ambience! Today the towpath has been upgraded and the canal forms one of the many park attractions. My drawing is of the lake.

19

THE FRONT FACADE of Ford Green Hall shows the various stages of its construction. In the centre is the original timber-framed hall, built in 1624 with a projecting porch and chamber above added a few years later. At either side are brick east and west wings added in 1734 and 1728 respectively

OLD OAK FURNITURE: much of the furniture in the hall is oak dating from the late 15th century onwards, to show the style of home the Ford family may have lived in. The rent table (left) dates from around 1540 whereas the children's high chair (right) would have been made circa 1680. Perhaps the most expensive of the many furnishings on display is a four poster bed with canopy over, dating from 1600~1650 which the Ford family located in the parlour. A long table of 1650 would have been the focus of family mealtimes and a wide variety of chests would have been used for storage.

FORD GREEN HALL

FORD GREEN HALL takes us back to an age before the Industrial Revolution when 'the Potteries' was farmland whose small towns and villages were connected by country lanes. Perhaps the oldest house in Stoke-on-Trent, Ford Green Hall is an Elizabethan gem, a manor house built for a Yeoman farmer with luxurious timber framing to reflect his wealth. Today the hall is a fascinating folk museum in the care of the City Council, displayed as a family home as it would have been in the 17th and 18th centuries.

THE DOVECOTE at Ford Green Hall was probably built in the early 18th century to provide a source of both fresh meat for the table and manure for the farm.

HUGH FORD built the timber framed Ford Green Hall in 1624. His family first appear in local records in 1293, and by the 17th century enjoyed status and wealth sufficient to build this hall.

FROM FORD GREEN TO BURSLEM...... Pottery has been made in North Staffordshire since at least the first century AD, and flourished as a farmhouse industry from then on. Using clay brought to the surface by their ploughs, and local wood to fire their kilns, farmers created coarse pottery, most notably butter pots for the butter market in Uttoxeter. It was in Burslem that earthenware manufacture first moved from the farmhouse into small commercial potteries. Here, in this hilltop town, good quality clay and coal both appear near the surface; indeed it is said that coal used to outcrop in the cellar of the Red Lion Inn (next door to 'Big House'). The Adams family had been making pots in Burslem since at least 1448, and by 1762, when Josiah Wedgwood was still in the early years of his career, there were already 150 separate potteries in the Burslem area. The residents of Ford Green Hall would have known the Burslem pottery industry, but could they predict its eventual scale?......

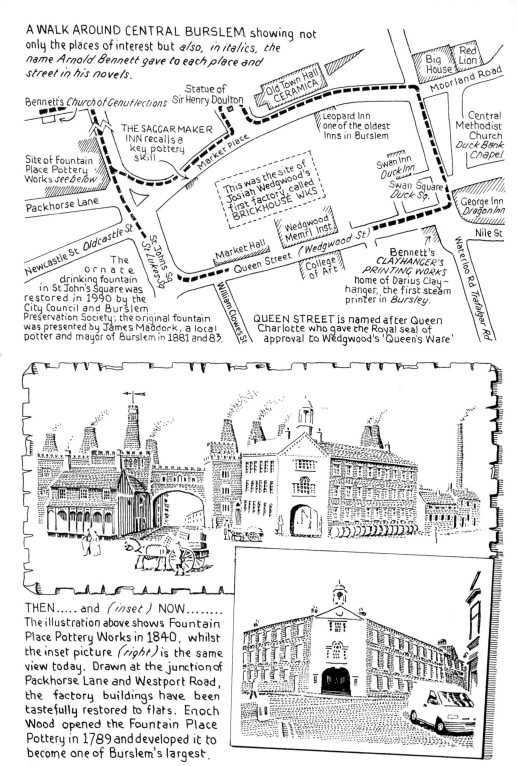

A WALK AROUND CENTRAL BURSLEM, showing not only the places of interest but *also, in italics, the name Arnold Bennett gave to each place and street in his novels.*

Big House
Red Lion
Moorland Road
Old Town Hall CERAMICA
Statue of Sir Henry Doulton
Bennett's *Church of Genuflections*
Leopard Inn one of the oldest Inns in Burslem
Central Methodist Church *Duck Bank Chapel*
THE SAGGAR MAKER INN recalls a key pottery skill
Market Place
Site of Fountain Place Pottery Works *see below*
Swan Inn *Duck Inn*
This was the site of Josiah Wedgwood's first factory called BRICKHOUSE WKS
Swan Square *Duck Sq.*
George Inn *Dragon Inn*
Packhorse Lane
Nile St
Newcastle St   Oldcastle St
St Johns Sq   St Lukes Sq
Market Hall
Wedgwood Meml Inst
Queen Street   *(Wedgwood St)*
College of Art
Bennett's *CLAYHANGER'S PRINTING WORKS* home of Darius Clayhanger, the first steam printer in *Bursley.*
Waterloo Rd   Trafalgar Rd

The ornate drinking fountain in St John's Square was restored in 1990 by the City Council and Burslem Preservation Society; the original fountain was presented by James Maddock, a local potter and mayor of Burslem in 1881 and 83.

William Clowes St

QUEEN STREET is named after Queen Charlotte who gave the Royal seal of approval to Wedgwood's 'Queen's Ware'

THEN..... and *(inset)* NOW........
The illustration above shows Fountain Place Pottery Works in 1840, whilst the inset picture *(right)* is the same view today. Drawn at the junction of Packhorse Lane and Westport Road, the factory buildings have been tastefully restored to flats. Enoch Wood opened the Fountain Place Pottery in 1789 and developed it to become one of Burslem's largest.

22

CENTRAL BURSLEM

1/4 mile. Terrain: street walking.

WHEN THE WRITER ARNOLD BENNETT found fame as a journalist in London, he never forgot his roots in Burslem. Indeed the town provided the inspiration for his most famous novels ~ Anna of the Five Towns *(1902)*, The Old Wives' Tale *(1908)* and the Clayhanger series *(1902~8)*. Around the town red plaques denote the locations which feature in his stories. But Burslem has another claim to fame ~ as "Mother of the Potteries" it was the first of the 'six towns' to convert its flourishing farmhouse pottery tradition into industrial scale production. Josiah Wedgwood built his first factory here, near his family's existing pottery which lay behind 'Big House' ~ the family home. Here, we tour the town centre, rich in history and splendid buildings.

Arnold Bennett 1867~1931

LEOPARD HOTEL ~ is one of the oldest in Burslem, built in the early 18th century. It was here, in March 1765, that a group of entrepreneurs including Josiah Wedgwood first met and agreed to sponsor the building of the Trent and Mersey Canal.

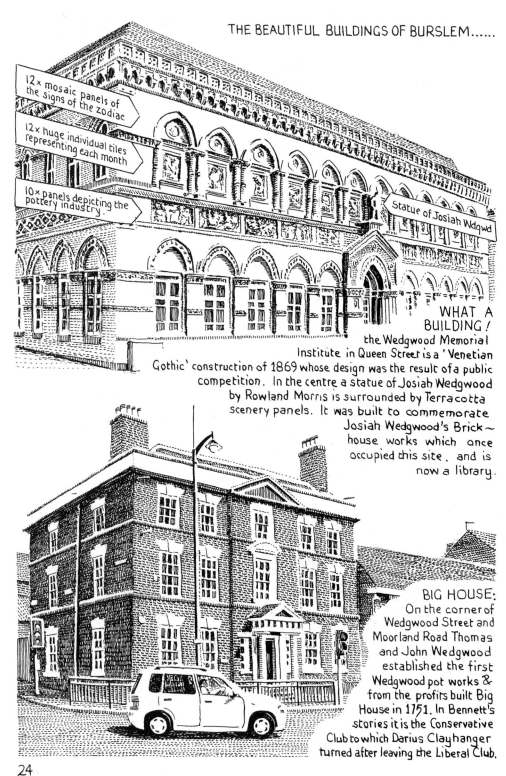

12 x mosaic panels of the signs of the zodiac

12 x huge individual tiles representing each month

10 x panels depicting the pottery industry.

Statue of Josiah Wdgwd

WHAT A BUILDING!
the Wedgwood Memorial Institute in Queen Street is a 'Venetian Gothic' construction of 1869 whose design was the result of a public competition. In the centre a statue of Josiah Wedgwood by Rowland Morris is surrounded by Terracotta scenery panels. It was built to commemorate Josiah Wedgwood's Brick—house works which once occupied this site. and is now a library.

BIG HOUSE:
On the corner of Wedgwood Street and Moorland Road Thomas and John Wedgwood established the first Wedgwood pot works & from the profits built Big House in 1751. In Bennett's stories it is the Conservative Club to which Darius Clayhanger turned after leaving the Liberal Club.

24

THE STATUE of Sir Henry Doulton stands guard outside Burslem's magnificent Italianate Old Town Hall, opened in 1857 to enormous acclaim. It was here that Arnold Bennett set his prestigious Countess of Chell's Ball in the five towns novel 'the Card'~set into a film starring Sir Alec Guiness with many locations filmed in Burslem. In 'The Old Wives' Tale' the head of the Baines family checked his watch each day by setting it to the Town Hall Chimes. The Hall is now an interactive museum of the pottery industry ~CERAMICA~ where one can learn how clay becomes china with lots of hands on activities. Award winning museum.

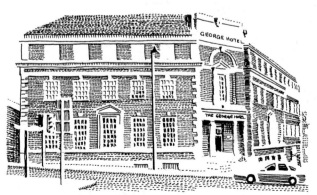

THE GEORGE HOTEL on the corner of Waterloo Road and Nile Street was Bennett's 'Dragon Hotel' in his Clayhanger novels. Recently refurbished the George is now a traditional luxury hotel with a restaurant appropriately called.........'Bennetts'.

Then on to Apedale Country Park.....

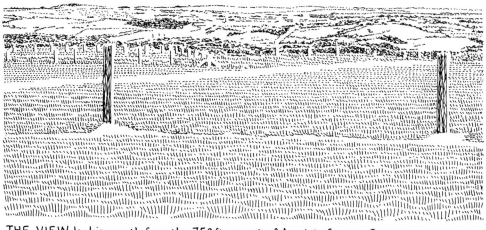

THE VIEW looking north from the 750ft summit of Apedale Country Park towards Bosley Cloud. the Roaches and the 'Matterhorn-like` peak of Shutlingsloe. 'Apedale Community Country Park' was reclaimed from open cast mining in 1995 and is now a recreational space rich in wooded valleys, pools and exposed hilltops commanding fine views. Amongst the diverse wildlife is a project to support the Great Crested Newt *(illustrated)*, and as part of the Staffordshire Biodiversity Action Plan the park also supports skylark, lapwing and grey partridges in its grassland areas and water vole along the course of the Lymebrook. The park is open for walking throughout the year.

APEDALE HERITAGE CENTRE

was created at the site of Apedale Mine to bring the story of mineral extraction to life. Highlight of the visit is a trip down the mine to see the coal seam and experience the life underground, but the museum traces the area's past back to pre-historic times. The Roman display includes part of a large 1st century building discovered in nearby Holditch in 1998. Cafe, shop and free parking.

APEDALE COUNTRY PARK

A SEVEN TONNE PITHEAD WHEEL at the summit of Apedale Country Park reminds us of its industrial history. Coal was probably first mined here by the Romans when miners from garrisons at Chesterton and Holditch probably sent coal to fire the Roman pottery kilns which have been found nearby. In more modern times Apedale became a drift mine employing, at its peak, 200 people and extracting nearly 2,000 tonnes of coal a week. Rail links connected Apedale to Holditch and Silverdale collieries where the coal was washed. Worked by the NCB until November 1969 and then by private operators, Apedale Colliery closed in 1994. The Romans were also, probably, the first to make iron in Apedale but it was the invention of the Blast Furnace which allowed the industry to fully develop. In the 19th century Apedale became one of the biggest centres of iron production in Britain, employing 3,000, but by the 1920's rising costs put the industry into decline and the ironworks closed altogether when the owner lost his fortune in the Wall Street crash. Sir Nigel Gresley built one of England's first canals here, but it was never linked up to the main network.

This stretch of the Macclesfield Canal is the boundary between Staffordshire and Cheshire.

Congleton Road A34

Red Bull Aqueduct→

A50 Liverpool Road East

Pool Lock Aqueduct→

Crossover Bridge→

barge workshop

A34 to Newcastle

moorings

Trent and Mersey Canal

← Railway line to Crewe

Macclesfield Canal

BARGING UNDER THE HILL: the entrances to the two Harecastle canal tunnels, each 1¾ miles long and 45 minutes 'sailing' time for barges to reach the other end. To the right is Brindley's tunnel of 1766, now abandoned and replaced by Thomas Telford's slightly wider and longer tunnel of 1827. Traffic is one way at a time, in alternating convoys controlled by the keepers at both ends. Long standing subsidence has reduced headroom to just 6 feet in the centre of the tunnel and a series of chains hanging over the entrance profiles the lowest point as a warning to inexperienced bargees!

KIDSGROVE AND THE HARECASTLE TUNNELS

2 miles. Terrain: canal towpath, paths and woodland

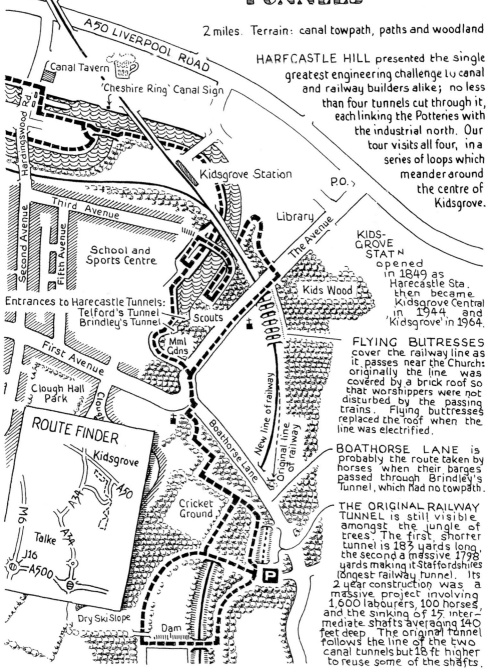

HARECASTLE HILL presented the single greatest engineering challenge to canal and railway builders alike; no less than four tunnels cut through it, each linking the Potteries with the industrial north. Our tour visits all four, in a series of loops which meander around the centre of Kidsgrove.

KIDSGROVE STAT'N opened in 1849 as Harecastle Sta. then became Kidsgrove Central in 1944 and 'Kidsgrove' in 1964.

FLYING BUTTRESSES cover the railway line as it passes near the Church: originally the line was covered by a brick roof so that worshippers were not disturbed by the passing trains. Flying buttresses replaced the roof when the line was electrified.

BOATHORSE LANE is probably the route taken by horses when their barges passed through Brindley's Tunnel, which had no towpath.

THE ORIGINAL RAILWAY TUNNEL is still visible amongst the jungle of trees. The first, shorter tunnel is 183 yards long, the second a massive 1798 yards making it Staffordshire's longest railway tunnel. Its 2 year construction was a massive project involving 1,600 labourers, 100 horses, and the sinking of 15 intermediate shafts averaging 140 feet deep. The original tunnel follows the line of the two canal tunnels but 18 ft higher to reuse some of the shafts.

Map labels:
A50 LIVERPOOL ROAD
Canal Tavern
'Cheshire Ring' Canal Sign
Hardingswood Rd.
Kidsgrove Station
P.O.
Library
The Avenue
Second Avenue
Third Avenue
Fifth Avenue
School and Sports Centre
Entrances to Harecastle Tunnels: Telford's Tunnel Brindley's Tunnel
Scouts
Kids Wood
Mml Gdns
First Avenue
Clough Hall Park
Clough
New line of railway
Original line of railway
Boathorse Lane
ROUTE FINDER
Kidsgrove
A50
A34
A34
M6
J16
A500
Talke
Cricket Ground
P
Dry Ski Slope
Dam

29

REACH FOR THE SKY: the walk passes Kidsgrove Cricket Club ~ established in 1877 ~ whose badge includes a Spitfire to honour its designer R J Mitchell, who grew up nearby.

MACCLESFIELD CANAL: part of this walk follows the towpath of the southern end of the Macclesfield Canal ~ a beautiful waterway which runs for 26 miles through 17 locks from Kidsgrove to Marple. Its whole length forms part of the famous 'Cheshire Ring'.

WHO SAYS FLYOVERS ARE A 20th CENTURY INVENTION? As the Macclesfield Canal leaves Kidsgrove it passes over two massive aqueducts ~ Pool Lock Aqueduct carries it over the Trent and Mersey Canal then Red Bull Aqueduct over the busy A50. A tablet on each, boldly inscribed with Roman lettering, allows us to date them 1827 and 1828 respectively. Nearly 200 years old and still in active use!

'PARADISE OF THE POTTERIES': Clough Hall was home to a wealthy mine owner until the early 1900's when it became a popular local theme park.

THE SIMPLE SEMICIRCULAR ARCH of Brindley's 1766 canal tunnel belies the incredible engineering feat involved in its construction. Fifteen vertical shafts were sunk: two headings from each and one at each end meant that thirty two headings were being worked simultaneously, yet it still took 11 years to complete due to the hard Millstone Grit, fire damp from nearby coal seams and underground springs. The absence of a towpath meant it took two hours to 'leg' barges through and the resulting congestion proved unacceptable. Thomas Telford was asked to design a second, parallel tunnel which opened in April 1827 and which is still in use today.

A LONDON BOUND EXPRESS powers over the Trent and Mersey Canal, heading towards the Harecastle Tunnel. During electrification in the 1960's the original railway tunnel was found to be in poor physical condition and required expensive repairs, so the 'Harecastle diversion' was constructed. At 2 miles long the new line bypassed the three tunnels on the old line, but required the creation of a new tunnel ~ the fourth to pierce beneath Harecastle Hill.

BEWARE THE KIDSGROVE BOGGART! The headless apparition of a woman murdered in one of the canal tunnels has been known to appear in these parts.

POOL LOCK drawn from the Macclesfield Canal. This is the highest 'summit' lock on the T&M raising it to 408ft ready for the Harecastle Tunnel.

SPANISH ARMADA: Mow Cop was one of a chain of beacons lit during the reign of Elizabeth I to warn of imminent invasion by the Spanish Armada. On 29 July 1981 it was again host to a beacon, by order of Buckingham Palace, to commemorate the wedding of Prince Charles to Diana Spencer. Charles lit the first beacon in Hyde Park before a chain of beacons rippled around the country. A flare from a beacon on The Wrekin was intended to signal the lighting of the Mow Cop beacon, but fog meant the message was relayed by radio.

WHEN MOW COP CASTLE was given to the National Trust in 1937, 10,000 Methodists marked the occasion with a rally on the hill. They were celebrating a similar rally at Mow Cop Castle 130 years earlier which gave birth to 'Primitive Methodism'. In 1807 Hugh Bourne from Stoke and William Clowes from Burslem organised a series of rallies in wild and isolated places to support their campaign for a more simple form of Methodist worship. At the height of its popularity, Primitive Methodism had some 5,000 Churches and 100,000 members but re-united with mainstream Methodism in 1932.

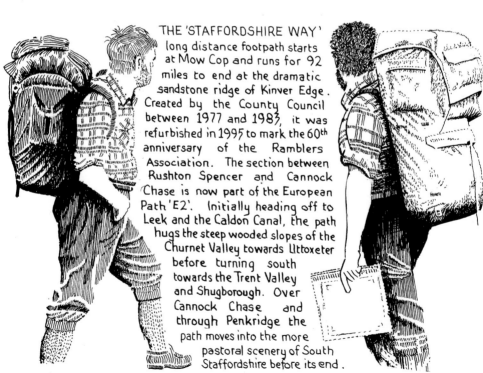

THE 'STAFFORDSHIRE WAY' long distance footpath starts at Mow Cop and runs for 92 miles to end at the dramatic sandstone ridge of Kinver Edge. Created by the County Council between 1977 and 1983, it was refurbished in 1995 to mark the 60th anniversary of the Ramblers Association. The section between Rushton Spencer and Cannock Chase is now part of the European Path 'E2'. Initially heading off to Leek and the Caldon Canal, the path hugs the steep wooded slopes of the Churnet Valley towards Uttoxeter before turning south towards the Trent Valley and Shugborough. Over Cannock Chase and through Penkridge the path moves into the more pastoral scenery of South Staffordshire before its end.

MOW COP CASTLE

PERCHED ON TOP OF A MASSIVE STONE OUTCROP *(Yoredale Rocks)* which itself tops a 1,100 ft high limestone escarpment, Mow Cop Castle is a folly built in 1754 by Randle Wilbraham 1 to enhance the view from Rode Hall, some two miles distant on the Cheshire Plain. It is one of England's earliest examples of artificially creating the ruin of a castle. The carboniferous Yoredale Rocks are amongst the oldest in the area, mined for coal to the east and for limestone on their western flank: the nearby Old Man of Mow is a pinnacle created by miners quarrying around it.

FROM THE CASTLE RAMPARTS there is a 360° view across five counties. This sketch looks towards Knypersley *(site of the next tour)* although it was a little misty on this day.

The panoramic views from Hill Top.....

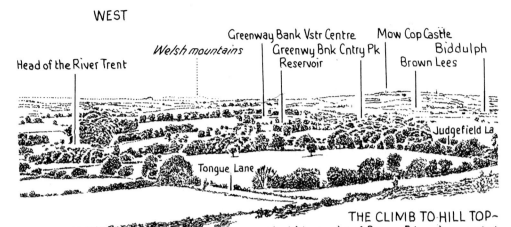

WEST

Head of the River Trent — Welsh mountains — Greenway Bank Vstr Centre — Greenwy Bnk Cntry Pk — Reservoir — Mow Cop Castle — Biddulph — Brown Lees — Judgefield La — Tongue Lane

THE CLIMB TO HILL TOP— the highest point of Brown Edge, is rewarded with magnificent views across most of North Staffordshire. Looking west, this drawing covers the area of this tour although Knypersley Reservoir is hidden in the valley. Beyond lies Mow Cop, the Cheshire Plain and ~ on a clear day ~ Snowdonia.

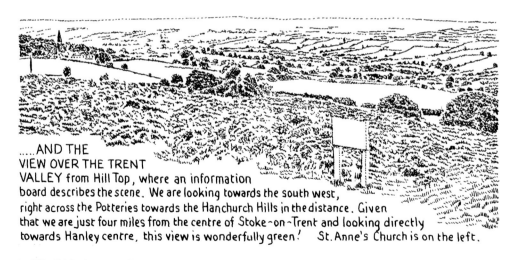

.....AND THE VIEW OVER THE TRENT VALLEY from Hill Top, where an information board describes the scene. We are looking towards the south west, right across the Potteries towards the Hanchurch Hills in the distance. Given that we are just four miles from the centre of Stoke-on-Trent and looking directly towards Hanley centre, this view is wonderfully green! St. Anne's Church is on the left.

HISTORIC HILL TOP: 'Hill Top' is the highest and oldest part of Brown Edge, an attractive upland village sitting high on a south westerly spur of the Pennine Chain. Its origins are rooted in coal mining ~ before the industrial revolution few people lived on this windy ridge, but the population grew with the opening of several local mines. "Brown" in the name is thought to refer to the uncultivated land, which can still be seen around the summit ~ on *Marshes Hill Common* from where the views above were drawn. What a contrast with the more fertile land in the Trent Valley below where many of the farmhouses date from circa 1600.

KNYPERSLEY RESERVOIR, HEAD OF THE RIVER TRENT AND BROWN EDGE

2 miles.   Terrain: field walking with a little road walking, with a gentle but long climb.

KNYPERSLEY RESERVOIRS ~ there are two of them ~ supply the Caldon and the Trent and Mersey canals with water, and this pleasant rural walk explores the aquatic history of the infant Trent Valley. After following the feeder canal through fields the route climbs towards 'Hill Top'~ the highest point of Brown Edge at 940ft above sea level ~ to enjoy stunning views through 360°. The upper of the two Knypersley reservoirs ~ 'The Serpentine'~ forms the focus of Greenway Bank Country Park which is featured after this walk.

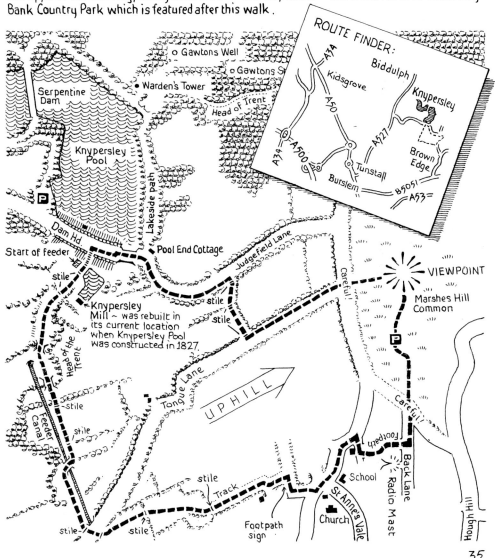

A SOLITARY FISHERMAN at Knypersley Pool, designed by civil engineering giant Thomas Telford and opened in 1827 to supply to the Caldon Canal and from there into the Trent and Mersey Canal. There are two reservoirs here, separated by a small dam. The 'Serpentine Pool' is the higher of the two and enjoys the accolade of being Britain's first reservoir, first filled in 1783 but eventually found to be inadequate.

KEEPING A BUSY CANAL SUPPLIED WITH WATER......
During the summer months the Trent and Mersey Canal loses water downhill by the 'lockfull' so requires a constant flow into its summit level between Etruria and Harecastle. The Caldon Canal was created with this objective in mind; joining the Trent and Mersey at its summit level it brings fresh water from three reservoirs at Rudyard Lake, Knypersley Pool and Stanley Pool near Stockton Brook. Water for the Trent and Mersey also feeds down the Macclesfield Canal with water from the two Macclesfield Reservoirs, Sutton and Bosley, and also from the Upper Peak Forest reservoirs at Combs and Toddbrook.

WATER cascades into the square gauging pool on the downstream side of the dam. A slate weir runs along three sides of the pool, dividing the flow between the Caldon Canal feed and the infant River Trent.

ST. ANNE'S CHURCH in Brown Edge was built in 1844 and contains stained glass by William Morris and Sir Edward Burne-Jones. The characterful steeple was donated in 1854 by Hugh Henshall Williamson - *see Greenway Bank Country Park on the next page.*

MIGHTY RIVER: the River Trent rises above Knypersley Pool in Biddulph Moor then flows 171 miles until it enters the North Sea beyond Scunthorpe. It is the third longest river in England, after the Thames and the Severn; and has come to form the dividing line between the north and south of England.

In 47AD the Roman invasion force reached the River Trent and consolidated their position for 32 years before moving further north in 79AD. Wulfhere, the 7th century King of Mercia *(see feature 1)*, navigated the river to Bury Bank near Stone from where he ruled his kingdom. St Modwen, the Irish missionary, founded a monastery on an island at Burton-on-Trent in 900AD, and the Benedictine Burton Abbey was founded in 1000AD

Scunthorpe

Gainsborough

Biddulph Moor
Knypersley Pool

Stoke-on-Trent

River Trent

Newark
Nottingham
Burton-on-Trent

The River Trent flows through five counties on its journey to the sea, and is one of only two English rivers with a tidal bore, the other being the River Severn.

Standing at Hill Top, the valley at your feet gives birth to this great British river. An old monument near the village of Biddulph Moor marks its source, feeding into Knypersley Pool then on to the Potteries.

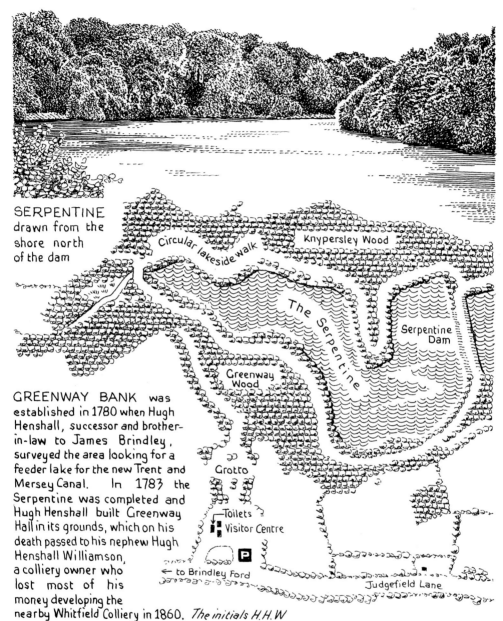

SERPENTINE drawn from the shore north of the dam

Circular lakeside walk

Knypersley Wood

The Serpentine

Serpentine Dam

Greenway Wood

Grotto

Toilets

Visitor Centre

P

← to Brindley Ford

Judgefield Lane

GREENWAY BANK was established in 1780 when Hugh Henshall, successor and brother-in-law to James Brindley, surveyed the area looking for a feeder lake for the new Trent and Mersey Canal. In 1783 the Serpentine was completed and Hugh Henshall built Greenway Hall in its grounds, which on his death passed to his nephew Hugh Henshall Williamson, a colliery owner who lost most of his money developing the nearby Whitfield Colliery in 1860. *The initials H.H.W appear on a stone on the Serpentine Dam.* Next, the estate was bought by Robert Heath, whose family were giants of the local iron and coal industries; indeed Heath Ironworks were believed to be the world's greatest producers of bar iron in the early 20th century. Under the Heath family the estate prospered, and from 1873 to 1919 formed a part of the Biddulph Grange Estate. Eventually the mansion was vacated and offered for sale in 1971, but the fabric of the building had deteriorated to an extent which made demolition the only option. Greenway Bank's new owners were the County Council who, with much foresight ~ and an awful lot of money ~ restored the overgrown valley to create the Park we see today.

GREENWAY BANK COUNTRY PARK

Situated just five miles from the centre of the Potteries, Greenway Bank and its neighbour Knypersley Pool combine to make a woodland park which would not be out of place in the Lake District. 'The Serpentine'~ Britain's first reservoir - was created to supply water to the Trent and Mersey Canal *via the Caldon Canal*, and is now a nature lovers paradise. Gentle walks through the lakeside shrubberies, ablaze with rhododendrons in late Spring, give way to more energetic walks through the valley of Gawtons stone. Near the car park a visitor centre brings the park to life with guides to the nature trails; on view are a range of woodland and freshwater birds, foxes, badgers and water voles, dragonflies and a huge range of shrubs and trees.

Former fish hatchery 000

OLD LEAF: captures and directs water towards the Serpentine.

O Gawtons Well

■ Gawtons Stone

≡ Steps

● Warden's Tower

Waterfall

Knypersley Pool (British Waterways Board)

Hollins Wood

P

Lakeside Footpath

Dam Head

Pool End Cottage

A FEEDER CANAL runs two miles from Knypersley to Norton Green where it empties into the Caldon Canal; the main objective of the water supply, however, was the mighty Trent and Mersey canal in Etruria.

GAWTON'S STONE is so called after a man from Knypersley Hall was cured of the plague after living as a hermit under these strange, Cromlech-like, rocks.

39

THE LEEK BRANCH of the Caldon Canal opened in 1802 and forked north here at Hazelhurst Junction to run through dense woods and rolling fields to Leek, some 2¾ miles distant. Three miles of feeder canal then runs to the beautiful Rudyard Lake. Hazelhurst Junction has changed considerably since its original opening ~ Endon Basin ~ A on the map below is the surviving stump of the original course. The present layout derives from the opening of the Stoke-Leek railway in 1841; 'New Junction' was created and a new diversion for the through route to Froghall was dug, falling 26ft through three new locks. The Leek route follows the course of the old canal which then crossed over the main canal using the massive Hazelhurst aqueduct. The original Hazelhurst Junction ~ at 'A' on the map below ~ consisted of a triple staircase lock the route of which can still be imagined on the ground.

Stoke~Leek Railway

New Jnctn   Lock 10
          Lock 11
          &12

Endon Brook

B

steps
Hazelhurst Aqueduct
Hollybush Inn

Hazelhurst Wood

A Original Hazelhurst Junction with remains of triple staircase locks

Huntley Road

HOLLYBUSH INN: a popular venue alongside the towpath of the Caldon Canal at Denford.

ENGLAND'S HIGHEST CANAL

1½ miles. Terrain: canal towpath [...] a little road walking.

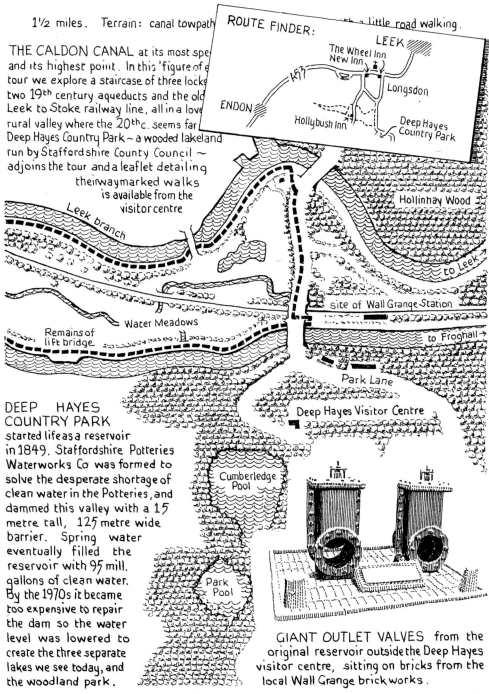

ROUTE FINDER:

LEEK
The Wheel Inn
New Inn
A53
ENDON
Longsdon
Hollybush Inn
Deep Hayes Country Park

THE CALDON CANAL at its most spe[...] and its highest point. In this 'figure of e[...] tour we explore a staircase of three locks[...] two 19th century aqueducts and the old [...] Leek to Stoke railway line, all in a love[...] rural valley where the 20th c. seems far [...] Deep Hayes Country Park ~ a wooded lakeland [...] run by Staffordshire County Council ~ adjoins the tour and a leaflet detailing the waymarked walks is available from the visitor centre

Leek branch

Hollinhay Wood

to Leek →

Water Meadows

site of Wall Grange Station

Remains of lift bridge

to Froghall →

Park Lane

Deep Hayes Visitor Centre

DEEP HAYES COUNTRY PARK

started life as a reservoir in 1849. Staffordshire Potteries Waterworks Co was formed to solve the desperate shortage of clean water in the Potteries, and dammed this valley with a 15 metre tall, 125 metre wide barrier. Spring water eventually filled the reservoir with 95 mill. gallons of clean water. By the 1970s it became too expensive to repair the dam so the water level was lowered to create the three separate lakes we see today, and the woodland park.

Cumberledge Pool

Park Pool

GIANT OUTLET VALVES from the original reservoir outside the Deep Hayes visitor centre, sitting on bricks from the local Wall Grange brickworks.

41

THE CALDON CANAL

runs 17 miles through 17 locks from the Trent and Mersey Canal at Etruria to Froghall. Completed in 1779 its original purpose was to carry limestone from the quarries at Caldon Low, but many other industries developed along its length *including the Cheddleton Flint Mill*. Hard to believe, then, that 200 years ago this peaceful valley was a major freight thoroughfare!

In 1811 the Caldon Canal was extended by 13 miles to Uttoxeter but this was subsequently filled in and in 1845 became a new railway. At Spath just outside Uttoxeter this line enjoyed the accolade of having the UK's first ever automatic train operated level crossing.'

Part of the justification for the Caldon Canal was its ability to supply water to the Trent and Mersey Canal. The largest of three feeder reservoirs was Rudyard Lake which connected to this canal via the 'Leek branch'

THE MASSIVE HAZELHURST AQUEDUCT carries the Leek Branch over the Caldon Canal. Note the person & dog for scale.

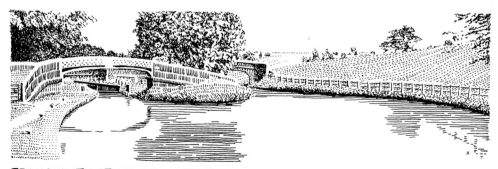

TRANQUILITY AT NEW JUNCTION: as the Leek branch goes off to the right, the main Caldon Canal starts its descent at Lock 10, left.

RURAL RAILWAY: a steam train passes Hazlehurst Locks in the early 1900's. The single track railway which weaves under the canal used to connect Leek with Stoke until passenger services were withdrawn in 1956. Technically it is a 6 mile line created in 1867 to link Leek Brook with Milton Junction with intermediate stations at Wall Grange, Endon, Stockton Brook and Milton. Our tour, and the canal, cross the railway via a cast iron aqueduct.

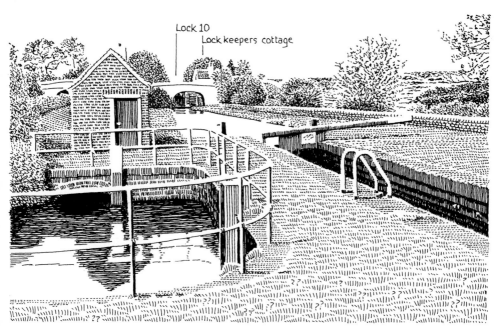

Lock 10
Lock keepers cottage

HAZLEHURST STAIRCASE: three locks ~ 10, 11 and 12 ~ lower the Caldon Canal by 26ft. A slightly technical sketch drawn at lock 11 to show the water saving side pound which collects half the water as the lock empties for re-use when it is refilled. Notice on the left bridge 1 of the Leek branch ~ which remains at the higher level throughout its length.

43

JUNGLE MAN: amongst the many people with good reason to remember Rudyard Lake were John Lockwood Kipling and Alice MacDonald who met here whilst on a works picnic in 1863. The story tells that they became so fond of this place that they named their first born son after it. Rudyard Kipling *illustrated* became one of England's most noted authors with such works as The Jungle Book and the poem 'If' but despite popular acclaim he declined many honours offered to him including a Knighthood and the Poet Laureateship. He did, however, accept the Nobel Prize for Literature in 1907, aged 42.

VISITOR ATTRACTION Today the 168 acre Rudyard Lake is a major leisure venue offering a variety of watersports, walking and cycling. Ornithologists flock here from across the country to see Rudyard's rich fauna, notably in the shallow waters and sand flats at its northern end. A visitor centre has been created at the dam head by converting a 150 year old boat house and a smart new toilet block and lakeside cafe complete the experience. Free parking is available at the Narrow Guage Railway station.

RAILWAY RESORT: in 1845 the North Staffordshire Railway Company opened its new line along the eastern shore of Rudyard Lake and developed Rudyard into a lakeside resort. Bank holiday excursion trains arrived from Leek every 15 minutes, and in 1877 20,000 people flocked here to see Captain Webb re-enact his famous channel swim across the lake. Today a narrow gauge steam railway offers a delightful 3 mile round trip from the free car park at Rudyard Station along the side of Rudyard Lake.

RUDYARD LAKE

WORKING RESERVOIR: encircled by wooded hills and surely one of England's most beautiful lakes, Rudyard is actually a reservoir constructed in 1799 to maintain the water level in the Caldon Canal. More than 200 years later it still performs the same function.

Lady of the Lake

LAKESIDE VIEW: a pleasant 5 mile walk circumnavigates the lake through scenery which is always wonderful and sometimes dramatic; indeed the *Staffordshire Way* runs along the shore. One of the waterside houses illustrated here is built out into the water and carries a statue known locally as the 'Lady of the Lake' *(illustrated from eastern shore)*

THE BLACK LION INN is said to be one of the oldest in Staffordshire. The view over the hills from the adjoining Churchyard is expansive, and well worth 'absorbing'.

THE 'OLD SCHOOL' TEA ROOMS is well placed for walkers at the top of Hollow Lane. A footpath from here climbs through the fields over to Deep Hayes Country Park.

CHEDDLETON

1½ miles.   Terrain: canal towpath, field walking and a few roads.

From Saxon beginnings, Cheddleton's rich history is closely linked to the River Churnet, the Caldon Canal and then the North Staffordshire Railway ~ now restored to steam as the Churnet Valley Railway. In a circular valley walk we explore all of this, including the twin waterwheels of Cheddleton's Flint Mill, climbing out of the valley to find the 14th century Parish Church, stocks, an ancient cross and a gorgeous countryside tea room.

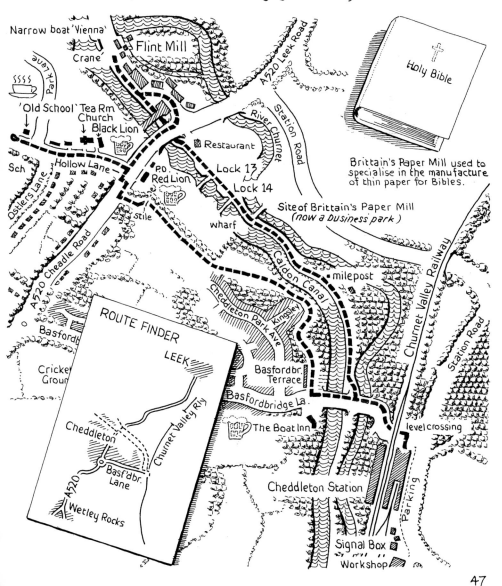

CHEDDLETON'S PARISH CHURCH of Edward the Confessor dates from the 12th century although the tower is Elizabethan ~ note the date 1574 on its south facing battlements. Further alterations were carried out in 1863 by Sir Gilbert Scott, the famous Gothic Revival architect responsible for the Albert Memorial in London. The richly decorated interior is well worth a visit ~ there is Victorian stained glass by Burne-Jones, William Morris and Ford Madox Brown, all of whom spent time in Leek learning the skill of dyeing cloth; indeed William Morris was a Churchwarden here. Outside the Lychgate with its saddleback roof was designed by Gilbert Scott Junior, as was the library and the old school. Near the Priest's Door in the Churchyard is a tombstone marked N.T. 1679.

The Elizabethan tower of Cheddleton's Parish Church.

Saxon Cross in the Churchyard

CHEDDLETON is an ancient village, sitting on top of a rocky spur overlooking a medieval ford across the River Churnet. From this ford the Leek to Stafford road climbed the narrow sunken lane known today as Hollow Lane to pass the small village huddled around its Parish Church. The Domesday Book of 1087 reveals the Lord of the Manor was Hugh Lupus, Earl of Chester. By the 13th century we know there was a corn mill on the site now occupied by the Flint Mill. In the centre of this ancient village we can still see the stocks (opposite the Black Lion) and the pound for stray animals.